«Managers do things right.
Leaders do the right thing.»

© JFederer – All Rights Reserved

1
«Knowing stuff is intelligence.
Knowing what we don't know is wisdom.»

The Elephant in the Room

The term «The Elephant in the Room» refers to a question, problem, solution, or controversial issue that is obvious to everyone who knows about the situation but is deliberately ignored because to do otherwise would cause great embarrassment, sadness, or arguments or is simply taboo.

The idiom can imply a value judgment that the issue ought to be discussed openly. It can also be an acknowledgment that the problem is there and not going to go away by itself.

«Knowing stuff is intelligence.
Knowing what we don't know is wisdom.»

April 2021

Recently I attended a Zoom call with a bunch of Silicon Valley founders. We were discussing exit strategies from their company's Covid-gridlock when one of us asked a brilliant question:

«Folks, what did we choose to do in the past instead of preparing for a pandemic we all knew was gonna hit humanity one day?»

There was an awkward silence at first. But then, these wise ladies and clever gentlemen named a ton of tried and approved business gambits that got us to where we are today.

As a result, these leaders decided to change course. They were licensing out their global business model into local markets, closing real-estate leases in flagship markets up to 50% below pre-covid market price. And they raised their revenue by 200% ever since this one question has been asked.

This is the stuff true leaders are made of. Managers have all the answers. Leaders ask the most innovative questions.

It takes knowledge to innovate, but it takes a beginner's mind to be original. This is creativity's evil twist. We aspire for knowledge, when all along, the fertile ground for innovation is the unknown.

«Knowing stuff is intelligence.
Knowing what we don't know is wisdom.»

Asking smart questions is the single-most-important magic bullet to transform from the intelligence of knowing to the wisdom of knowing what we don't know. To shift from being an imitating manager to serving as an innovating leader.

When framed right, a brilliant question can change the course of an entire operation, a life, a change initiative, or a family.

So often, we simply dole out words of wisdom, reinforcing knowledge from the past that acts as a roadblock for discovering creative solutions for the future. But every time we meet a challenge with the stuff we know, we give away an opportunity to innovate. Resisting the transformation into the unknown. But it's in that uncharted space where innovation happens.

In my career, I had the opportunity to experience some of the brightest leaders and talent in the space of tech, human sciences, art, publishing, sports, and entertainment. What always struck me about exceptional leaders is that even though they rely on vast experience, they rarely dole out words of wisdom. Their number one skill is to ask the most brilliant questions.

In this book, «Finding the Elephant in the Room,» I collected 444 brilliant questions I witnessed successful leaders ask. You may pose them to yourself, your clients, your superior, your team, your investor, your friends, or your partner. You may work through this book cover to cover or flip through the pages, randomly stopping

«Knowing stuff is intelligence.
Knowing what we don't know is wisdom.»

anywhere. The questions are divided into chapters to discover yourself, your career, goals, and network.

Blessings,
J «Fed» Federer,
Poop Unicorn

(Poop Unicorn = a person that is different and may be considered evil by conventional thinkers.)

«Knowing stuff is intelligence.
Knowing what we don't know is wisdom.»

The Design Of Brilliant Questions:

1. A brilliant question is open-ended, bestowing the opportunity for an elementary shift in the consciousness of your plan.

2. A brilliant question does not conduct a value judgment. (such as «why»)

3. It's improbable for you to know the answer to a brilliant question.

4. Brilliant questions don't assess a problem, as evaluation is an act of oppression.

5. The fewer words you use, the more significant the impact of your question will be.

«Knowing stuff is intelligence.
Knowing what we don't know is wisdom.»

Self-Discovery	8
Career-Discovery	64
Goal-Discovery	78
Network-Discovery	120

«Knowing stuff is intelligence.
Knowing what we don't know is wisdom.»

Self-Discovery

«Knowing stuff is intelligence.
Knowing what we don't know is wisdom.»

1.
«How does your life compare with what you expected it to be?»

«Knowing stuff is intelligence.
Knowing what we don't know is wisdom.»

2.
What would you like to change about yourself?

3.
What's wrong with the way you are?

4.
What is your theme for the next twelve months in one word?

5.
What do you know for sure?

6.
What do you love most about your life right now?

«Knowing stuff is intelligence.
Knowing what we don't know is wisdom.»

7.
If someone was to really hurt your feelings, what would they say?

8.
What's been your high point of this day?

9.
What choices led you to this place?

10.
What's your favorite way of sabotaging yourself?

11.
If there were only three rules that everyone would have to follow, what would they be?

«Knowing stuff is intelligence.
Knowing what we don't know is wisdom.»

12.
What needs to change about who you are for your life to go where it needs to go?

13.
What would your life be like if you only pleased yourself?

14.
What do you secretly know you need to say 'No' to?

15.
Who are you now, and who would you like to become?

16.
How have you held yourself back?

«Knowing stuff is intelligence.
Knowing what we don't know is wisdom.»

17.
What makes this a good day?

18.
When was the last time you did something 'big' just for you?

19.
What's one thing you need to move to the next level that you currently don't have?

20.
What needs in the world are you moved to meet?

21.
What is something you love to do?

«Knowing stuff is intelligence.
Knowing what we don't know is wisdom.»

22.
«What actions didn't you take that led to this situation?»

14
«Knowing stuff is intelligence.
Knowing what we don't know is wisdom.»

23.
What's the best thing
about your life right now?

24.
Consider the last week. What did you go
out of your way to do and not do?

25.
What's your dream for this lifetime?

26.
If you were to live your life fully, what is
the first change you would make?

27.
What do you want the headline
of your life to be?

«Knowing stuff is intelligence.
Knowing what we don't know is wisdom.»

28.
What would you like more of in your life?

29.
What would you like less of in your life?

30.
Where do you see yourself going in a year?

31.
Write down your first achievement ever in life.

32.
What would you do if you didn't have to live with the consequences?

«Knowing stuff is intelligence.
Knowing what we don't know is wisdom.»

33.
«What about your situation is within your control?»

«Knowing stuff is intelligence.
Knowing what we don't know is wisdom.»

34.
What will you do in the next 24 hours?

35.
On a scale from one to ten, where do you see your life right now?

36.
If one burden could be removed from you in the next 30 days, what would that be?

37.
What are your current priorities?

38.
What's absolutely perfect about your current situation?

«Knowing stuff is intelligence.
Knowing what we don't know is wisdom.»

39.
How can you keep those good aspects while still moving towards change?

40.
What are three things you are regularly doing that don't serve or support you?

41.
Who would you be without your thoughts?

42.
What price have you already paid for these thoughts?

43.
What are the top opportunities that present themselves right now?

«Knowing stuff is intelligence.
Knowing what we don't know is wisdom.»

44.
«If you were to consider what's possible, instead of what's probable, how does that change things?»

«Knowing stuff is intelligence.
Knowing what we don't know is wisdom.»

45.
What were the biggest challenges in your life, and how did you overcome them?

46.
What would you love to have happened by the end of this hour?

47.
What's the best thing that happened this month in your sphere of influence?

48.
What are the three things that would make the biggest difference in your life?

49.
What are you ready to change?

«Knowing stuff is intelligence.
Knowing what we don't know is wisdom.»

50.
What are you tolerating and putting up with?

51.
What are the things you want to remove from your life?

52.
What are you not ready to change yet?

53.
How do you normally sabotage yourself?

54.
When are you unable to laugh at yourself?

«Knowing stuff is intelligence.
Knowing what we don't know is wisdom.»

55.
What are five essential strengths and three weaknesses you encounter daily?

56.
Where are you not respecting yourself right now?

57.
When do you give your power away and to whom?

58.
Where are you the solution?

59.
What do you want in life but don't have?

«Knowing stuff is intelligence.
Knowing what we don't know is wisdom.»

60.
«Is it the situation you need to change or is it the way you respond to it?»

61.
What is it that you believe that keeps you from being fully yourself?

62.
If you could only take three things into a difficult, possibly dangerous situation, which are the things you absolutely must have?

63.
What do you have in your life, but don't want it?

64.
If you had to guess your life purpose from looking at your life to date, what would it be?

«Knowing stuff is intelligence.
Knowing what we don't know is wisdom.»

65.
What do you lack?

66.
If you secretly knew the way forward from here, what would it be?

67.
What must you do going forward?

68.
Which action leaps out at you today?

69.
Suppose you had all the information you needed; what would be the next step?

«Knowing stuff is intelligence.
Knowing what we don't know is wisdom.»

70.
«Write down who you are, without using labels, roles, or job descriptions.»

«Knowing stuff is intelligence.
Knowing what we don't know is wisdom.»

71.
Let's imagine you're really excited.
What would you do?

72.
If you were at your best,
what would you do right now?

73.
What do you most need that you
don't have to live a life of passion
and purpose?

74.
Where are you stopping short?

75.
What is a decision
you have been avoiding?

«Knowing stuff is intelligence.
Knowing what we don't know is wisdom.»

76.
«What would be the best question someone could ask you now?»

«Knowing stuff is intelligence.
Knowing what we don't know is wisdom.»

77.
What do you not want to be asked?

78.
If you secretly knew what was holding you back, what would it be?

79.
Imagine for a moment that your issues are resolved. How did you get there?

80.
What did you fail at or make a mistake on that needs recognition?

81.
What did you learn, and what are you proud of in how you handled it?

«Knowing stuff is intelligence.
Knowing what we don't know is wisdom.»

82.
What have you achieved that has surprised you?

83.
What haven't you admitted out loud yet?

84.
If, overnight, a miracle happened and you got unstuck, who would you be?

85.
What's the problem in a nutshell?

86.
And what's the problem in one word?

87.
What are you avoiding?

«Knowing stuff is intelligence.
Knowing what we don't know is wisdom.»

88.
What do you get out of having difficulties?

89.
What research could you do to help you find the first step towards fulfillment?

90.
If you got really radical today, stopped fearing the consequences and launched out to be what you were born to be. What would you be doing?

91.
What difference could make the difference?

«Knowing stuff is intelligence.
Knowing what we don't know is wisdom.»

92.
«Picture yourself five years from now. Look back. What was the turning point?»

«Knowing stuff is intelligence.
Knowing what we don't know is wisdom.»

93.
What do you think your feelings might be trying to protect you from?

94.
What obstacles have you run into in the past?

95.
What would you do if others never changed?

96.
What is the positive intention behind your behavior?

97.
What do your beliefs do for you?

«Knowing stuff is intelligence.
Knowing what we don't know is wisdom.»

98.
«What do you need to stop saying 'Yes' to?»

«Knowing stuff is intelligence.
Knowing what we don't know is wisdom.»

99.
Is dissatisfaction driving you, or is it a desire to pursue something new?

100.
Where could you be more forgiving and understanding of yourself?

101.
What is the positive intention behind keeping a self-limiting belief?

102.
How would your life be different if you were to let go of your beliefs?

103.
How would your life be different if you fully trusted yourself?

«Knowing stuff is intelligence.
Knowing what we don't know is wisdom.»

104.
What has the lack of belief in yourself cost you?

105.
How does 'avoidance' affect your life?

106.
What's your hesitation?

107.
Who are you trying to please?

108.
For your life to be perfect, what would have to change?

109.
What's holding you back?

«Knowing stuff is intelligence.
Knowing what we don't know is wisdom.»

110.
«Suppose, just for a moment, you live in a world where fear and anxiety do not exist. What could you do now?»

111.
Write down some examples of how you have been getting in your way.

112.
What seems to confuse you?

113.
What might you be embarrassed to look at that could be stopping you from moving forward?

114.
What is frustrating about your progress?

115.
Where are you stuck and not moving forward?

«Knowing stuff is intelligence.
Knowing what we don't know is wisdom.»

116.
How can you satisfy your positive intentions without relying on self-limiting beliefs?

117.
How do you stand in your own way?

118.
What rules do you have about how you should behave that are getting in the way of you moving forward?

119.
What might you feel silly to say out loud?

120.
Where do you have unrealistic expectations of yourself?

«Knowing stuff is intelligence.
Knowing what we don't know is wisdom.»

121.
Do you have proof of your beliefs?

122.
What would happen if you
doubled your self-belief?

123.
Where do you think your thoughts
could be getting in the way?

124.
Where are you too hard on yourself?

125.
What is getting in the way
of living the life you want?

«Knowing stuff is intelligence.
Knowing what we don't know is wisdom.»

126.
Who do you admire? What specifically about them do you admire?

127.
What is your favorite activity, and why?

128.
What does it mean to you to have a wholesome and prosperous life?

129.
What would you stand up and fight for?

130.
What would you risk your reputation over?

131.
What's motivating you right now?

132.
«What have you tried so far?»

133.
What are you passionately pursuing?

134.
What is most important to you in your life?

135.
Think about the times when you have been delighted. What values were being met?

136.
What's your dream?

137.
What about this is important to you?

«Knowing stuff is intelligence.
Knowing what we don't know is wisdom.»

138.
What are some fundamental values you apply when you make important decisions?

139.
Think about one or two people who inspire you. What about them is inspiring?

140.
What excites and inspires you?

141.
Think about the times you got upset. What values were not being met?

142.
What can't you be with?

«Knowing stuff is intelligence.
Knowing what we don't know is wisdom.»

143.
«Look forward 20 years... you are attending a function where someone is giving a speech about you. What would you want them to say?»

144.
In which areas do you serve others freely?

145.
What drives you crazy?

146.
What were you made to do?

147.
What must you always do?

148.
What would not be like it is, had you not been part of it?

149.
What are you most excited about for the coming year?

«Knowing stuff is intelligence.
Knowing what we don't know is wisdom.»

150.
How would your life be different if you were to believe in yourself?

151.
What do you believe about your own ability to improve?

152.
What are you most proud of in your life?

153.
What are some unique skills you have?

154.
What special knowledge do you have?

155.
What do you like about yourself?

«Knowing stuff is intelligence.
Knowing what we don't know is wisdom.»

156.
«What do you get complimented for most?»

«Knowing stuff is intelligence.
Knowing what we don't know is wisdom.»

157.
What are three of your greatest strengths?

158.
If you were to totally and completely trust your intuition. What would you tell yourself?

159.
What are you most excited about for the coming year?

160.
What do you contribute that is unique?

«Knowing stuff is intelligence.
Knowing what we don't know is wisdom.»

161.
If you could travel back in time and meet yourself as a teenager, what three things would you tell yourself?

162.
Think of someone you admire and respect. How would you want to be described by them?

163.
What is your prevalent mood?

164.
Imagine you're 16 again. What advice would you give yourself today?

165.
What would you like to express more in your life?

«Knowing stuff is intelligence.
Knowing what we don't know is wisdom.»

166.
Where do you add stress to your life?

167.
Imagine you're 90 years old, happy, healthy, and you're sitting in your rocking chair. What advice would you give yourself right now?

168.
What does the way you're living your life say about you?

169.
What part of you is not being acknowledged?

170.
How much do you think you're worth?

«Knowing stuff is intelligence.
Knowing what we don't know is wisdom.»

171.
«What are you tolerating that needs to change for you to move forward?»

«Knowing stuff is intelligence.
Knowing what we don't know is wisdom.»

172.
What parts of yourself are you dying to let out?

173.
What parts of yourself are you denying?

174.
What is going to be your contribution to the world?

175.
What is out of harmony, and how do you restore it?

176.
What do you consider to be your role in this world?

«Knowing stuff is intelligence.
Knowing what we don't know is wisdom.»

177.
«When are you unable to laugh at yourself?»

«Knowing stuff is intelligence.
Knowing what we don't know is wisdom.»

178.
What do you yearn to do?

179.
Where do you need to take better care of yourself?

180.
Who are you now, and who will you need to become to complete your mission?

181.
If you could go back in time and meet any historical figure, who would it be, and why?

182.
What's your contribution to life?

«Knowing stuff is intelligence.
Knowing what we don't know is wisdom.»

183.
In which area of life do you long for more?

184.
What's bugging you right now?

185.
How full is your tank of love, friendships, fulfilling work, spirituality, and peace of mind?

186.
What is a big dream that you've always wanted to go after?

187.
What would help you the most over the next few weeks?

«Knowing stuff is intelligence.
Knowing what we don't know is wisdom.»

188.
«Write down five things you love about yourself.»

189.
In what ways do you inhibit your potential?

190.
What's the biggest challenge for you?

191.
What dreams do you have for the future?

192.
What is sapping your energy and motivation?

193.
What are you eager to leave behind?

194.
What are the three priorities this year?

«Knowing stuff is intelligence.
Knowing what we don't know is wisdom.»

195.
«What's your greatest asset?»

«Knowing stuff is intelligence.
Knowing what we don't know is wisdom.»

196.
What's missing in your life, the presence of which would have your life be more fulfilling?

197.
What's a priority for you right now?

198.
What's going on in life that's got your attention right now?

199.
What are the top three challenges you face right now?

200.
What's the most significant thing that's happened with you this year?

«Knowing stuff is intelligence.
Knowing what we don't know is wisdom.»

201.
What is the most significant thing that's happened in your life in the last month?

202.
Write down one joy and one sorrow that you've experienced this year.

203.
What is bringing you 80% of joy in life?

204.
What causes 80% of your stress in life?

205.
What bothers you the most?

206.
What hasn't been working for you?

«Knowing stuff is intelligence.
Knowing what we don't know is wisdom.»

207.
«Who would you like to be going forward?»

«Knowing stuff is intelligence.
Knowing what we don't know is wisdom.»

Career-Discovery

«Knowing stuff is intelligence.
Knowing what we don't know is wisdom.»

208.
«What makes your job significant?»

«Knowing stuff is intelligence.
Knowing what we don't know is wisdom.»

209.
Why do you care about your job?

210.
If you had unlimited resources, what would you do with them?

211.
Why did you take your job?

212.
What's the best thing about working with your company?

213.
How does your job bring out the best in you?

214.
How can you keep those good aspects while still moving towards change?

215.
What do you want to do in ten years?

216.
For your career to be perfect, what would have to change?

217.
If you could do anything at all, what would be your ideal career?

218.
What's good about your current situation?

«Knowing stuff is intelligence.
Knowing what we don't know is wisdom.»

219.
«If you won the lottery, what would you do?»

220.
If there was an outcome you were secretly looking for, what would it be?

221.
What were you made to do?

222.
What would you do if you weren't afraid?

223.
How well does your current role fit with your purpose and your natural strengths?

224.
How well does your current job supply what you truly want?

«Knowing stuff is intelligence.
Knowing what we don't know is wisdom.»

225.
What causes 80% of your stress in your current role?

226.
What causes 80% of your joy in your current role?

227.
What's been your favorite job in your career?

228.
What is something you love to do?

229.
What activities have heart and meaning for you?

«Knowing stuff is intelligence.
Knowing what we don't know is wisdom.»

230.
What are some fundamental values you apply when you make important decisions?

231.
What is most important to you in your career?

232.
What are you passionately pursuing?

233.
What's most important to you in a job?

234.
In which areas do you serve others freely?

«Knowing stuff is intelligence.
Knowing what we don't know is wisdom.»

235.
If you were an expert in the area of your career, what would you advise yourself to do?

236.
What skills and resources do you need to develop?

237.
What skills and resources do you already have?

238.
Has your career worked for you in the past?

239.
What's your USP?

240.
«What is the positive intention behind your career choices?»

«Knowing stuff is intelligence.
Knowing what we don't know is wisdom.»

241.
Suppose you had all the information you needed; what would be your next step?

242.
Let's imagine you're really excited. What would you do?

243.
How could you bring more creativity, fun, and joy to your career?

244.
How would your career be different if you fully trusted yourself?

245.
What special knowledge do you have?

«Knowing stuff is intelligence.
Knowing what we don't know is wisdom.»

246.
«What are you tolerating that needs to change in order for you to move forward?»

«Knowing stuff is intelligence.
Knowing what we don't know is wisdom.»

247.
How does 'avoidance' affect your career?

248.
What stands in the way of you being the best in your market niche?

249.
How would your career be different if you were to let go of your beliefs?

250.
What is an impossible option?

251.
What's the growing edge for you in your career these days?

«Knowing stuff is intelligence.
Knowing what we don't know is wisdom.»

«Knowing stuff is intelligence.
Knowing what we don't know is wisdom.»

Goal-Discovery

«Knowing stuff is intelligence.
Knowing what we don't know is wisdom.»

252.
«What would your goal be if you knew you could not fail?»

«Knowing stuff is intelligence.
Knowing what we don't know is wisdom.»

253.
If there was a goal you were secretly looking for, what would it be?

254.
What goals would you have if you didn't care what other people thought?

255.
What would your goal be if money were not an issue?

256.
What goals do you want more of in life?

257.
What goals do you want less of in life?

«Knowing stuff is intelligence.
Knowing what we don't know is wisdom.»

258.
If you had a magic wand and could change one thing about your goals immediately, what would that be?

259.
What would be the minimum and super-easy level goal to achieve?

260.
What's good about your current goals?

261.
How can you keep those good aspects while still moving towards change?

262.
What happens if you continue pursuing your present goals?

263.
If you could do anything at all, what would be your ideal goal?

264.
Who could you hang out with so achieving your goals becomes natural?

265.
What's the pay-off for doing nothing?

266.
What's the price for taking action?

267.
And what's the price
for not taking action?

268.
Who could help you
in reaching your goals?

269.
Who needs to know to make sure
you will meet your goals?

270.
Can you describe your
goals in one sentence?

271.
What are you not ready to do just yet?

«Knowing stuff is intelligence.
Knowing what we don't know is wisdom.»

272.
What could you do in the meantime?

273.
What could you stop doing?

274.
If you could only change one thing in your life, what would it be?

275.
What could you do as the very first step towards meeting your goal?

276.
What do you need to do before you do anything else?

«Knowing stuff is intelligence.
Knowing what we don't know is wisdom.»

277.
What would make sense this week?

278.
If you did nothing else in the next year, what three things would still make the year a success for you?

279.
What about your goals is within your control?

280.
What is the wackiest thing you could do to meet your goals?

281.
Which decision are you avoiding?

«Knowing stuff is intelligence.
Knowing what we don't know is wisdom.»

282.
Are your goals challenging enough to be exciting for you?

283.
How can you up the stakes and make your goals more interesting?

284.
Do you personally know anyone who already has your goal?

285.
What could you learn from them?

286.
What's a phone call you could make to move you towards your goals efficiently?

287.
«Is achieving your goals entirely under your own control?»

288.
What choices do you need to make to achieve your goals?

289.
What steps have you made towards larger goals that you need to acknowledge yourself for?

290.
How did you prevent yourself from completing your goals so far?

291.
What did you achieve instead of reaching your goals?

292.
How did that benefit you?

293.
«How can you make your goals measurable?»

294.
What did you choose to do
instead of pursuing your goals?

295.
Looking back, would you make
the same choice again?

296.
If your big picture goal
seems to be a bit of a stretch from
where you are now; write down a couple
of stepping stones along the way.

297.
What is the most significant change
you are willing to make today?

«Knowing stuff is intelligence.
Knowing what we don't know is wisdom.»

298.
What is one thing you will do immediately after reading this?

299.
What criteria could you use to measure your success?

300.
What would happen if you lowered your expectations?

301.
How will taking action towards your goals impact other people in your life?

302.
What if their response is not what you expect?

«Knowing stuff is intelligence.
Knowing what we don't know is wisdom.»

303.
What are five things you would love to do before you die?

304.
Who will you have to be to do them all?

305.
What are some important dreams you would like to pursue in the next five or ten years?

306.
And what do you secretly yearn for?

307.
How would your goals be different if you fully trusted yourself?

«Knowing stuff is intelligence.
Knowing what we don't know is wisdom.»

308.
«How could you rephrase your goals, so the outcome only depends on you and not on others?»

309.
If you were rich beyond your wildest dreams, how would you approach things differently?

310.
If you secretly didn't want to achieve your goal, what would you do instead?

311.
What one thing would you change in your sphere of influence?

312.
What areas of your life could be upgraded or tweaked?

313.
Are your goals still inspiring?

«Knowing stuff is intelligence.
Knowing what we don't know is wisdom.»

314.
What would be most helpful to focus on right now?

315.
What three things do you most want to achieve in the next 90 days?

316.
What, if you got it finished this week, would make you jump for joy?

317.
What specific goals would you like to meet this week?

318.
How would you feel about doubling your goals?

«Knowing stuff is intelligence.
Knowing what we don't know is wisdom.»

319.
What would you be disappointed you couldn't work on today?

320.
What are the top opportunities that present themselves right now?

321.
Imagine it's 90 days from now, and you achieved your goal. What was your contribution to this outcome?

322.
In which area could you make the most significant difference with the least amount of effort?

323.
How might your life be better with your goals?

324.
What would you do if others never changed?

325.
What is the price of change?

326.
Are you willing to pay the price?

327.
How might your life be worse with your goals?

«Knowing stuff is intelligence.
Knowing what we don't know is wisdom.»

328.
«What would happen if money were not an issue?»

«Knowing stuff is intelligence.
Knowing what we don't know is wisdom.»

329.
Can you complete your goals on your own, or do you need help from others?

330.
What needs to change so that you can achieve your goals on your own?

331.
What do you need to reach your goals that you don't have?

332.
What have you tried already?

333.
What have you already done towards your goals?

«Knowing stuff is intelligence.
Knowing what we don't know is wisdom.»

334.
What is the best possible outcome you could envision?

335.
What would a home run in your life look like this week?

336.
In the short term, what are the objectives you most want to improve?

337.
For your life to be perfect, what would have to change?

338.
What is your biggest challenge in the next twelve months?

«Knowing stuff is intelligence.
Knowing what we don't know is wisdom.»

339.
«If you are 90 years old and looking back at your life, what have you done to make you feel proud?»

«Knowing stuff is intelligence.
Knowing what we don't know is wisdom.»

340.
If you dared to say it aloud,
what would you make
happen in your life?

341.
Imagine you had all the time you
needed. What would you do?

342.
What is standing in the way of you
achieving the goals you want?

343.
What would have happened in six
months that your life is better
than you could have expected?

«Knowing stuff is intelligence.
Knowing what we don't know is wisdom.»

344.
«What would happen if you raised your expectations?»

«Knowing stuff is intelligence.
Knowing what we don't know is wisdom.»

345.
What two steps could you immediately take that would make the biggest difference in your current situation?

346.
If you got really radical today, stopped fearing the consequences, and launched out to be what you were born to be, what would you be doing?

347.
Why are your goals important to you?

348.
What one thing do you need to focus on to take this to the next level?

349.
Imagine you've just had an ideal week.
What three things did you complete?

350.
Name someone who has done
what you want to do.

351.
What changes would
make life an adventure?

352.
What one new skill would
make all the difference for you?

353.
What would it take for
your goals to be achieved?

«Knowing stuff is intelligence.
Knowing what we don't know is wisdom.»

354.
Let's imagine you're really excited.
What would you do?

355.
Suppose you had all the information you
needed; what would be the next step?

356.
If you were at your best,
what would you do right now?

357.
Where are you stopping short?

358.
If there was no 'history' or
'politics,' what could you do?

«Knowing stuff is intelligence.
Knowing what we don't know is wisdom.»

359.
«Have your goals worked for you in the past?»

«Knowing stuff is intelligence.
Knowing what we don't know is wisdom.»

360.
Imagine you're fully confident in your abilities; what could you do?

361.
What are three actions you could take that would make sense this month?

362.
Which actions can you see yourself taking this week?

363.
Think of someone successful you admire. What would they do next?

364.
What resources do you already have to achieve your goals?

«Knowing stuff is intelligence.
Knowing what we don't know is wisdom.»

365.
What resources have you used in the past that you could bring to the present time?

366.
Who could you tell about your goals that would support you in achieving them?

367.
On a scale of one to ten, how likely is it you will reach your goals in the time you set for yourself?

368.
What could move you towards your goals right now?

«Knowing stuff is intelligence.
Knowing what we don't know is wisdom.»

369.
«What can you accomplish today?»

370.
What are some useful qualities that would move you towards your goals?

371.
What resources, other than time and money, will you need to achieve your goals?

372.
If you were an expert in the area of your goals, what would you advise yourself to do?

373.
What three things could you do to support yourself?

«Knowing stuff is intelligence.
Knowing what we don't know is wisdom.»

374.
What stops you from doing more towards your goals?

375.
What would it be worth to you to change?

376.
What's an action you could take straight after reading this?

377.
What will you be doing differently that tells you you've completed your goal?

378.
What resources could you draw on to tackle your goals?

«Knowing stuff is intelligence.
Knowing what we don't know is wisdom.»

379.
«How does what others think and feel affect how you feel about your goals?»

380.
What are the outcomes when you achieve your goals?

381.
What is most important to you about your goals?

382.
If you reached your goals, how would you be different?

383.
How could you break down your overall goal into manageable milestones?

384.
What's your hesitation?

385.
«What goal would put a smile on your face? Now say this out loud and grin from ear to ear...»

«Knowing stuff is intelligence.
Knowing what we don't know is wisdom.»

386.
Who might be upset if you achieved your goals?

387.
Where do you feel stuck?

388.
What will be different as a result of you achieving your goals?

389.
Imagine what you want has occurred. What would people notice about you?

390.
What goals would you pursue if you didn't care what other people thought?

«Knowing stuff is intelligence.
Knowing what we don't know is wisdom.»

391.
What is the pain for you of not achieving your goals?

392.
How would your life be different if you were to let go of your beliefs?

393.
How does 'avoidance' affect your goals?

394.
In service of what do you set your goals?

395.
What would you most like to get out of the next hour?

«Knowing stuff is intelligence.
Knowing what we don't know is wisdom.»

396.
What might you be embarrassed to look at that could be stopping you from moving forward?

397.
What are you willing to sacrifice to work on your goals?

398.
What do you need to achieve in the next year to make sure your ten-year goal happens?

«Knowing stuff is intelligence.
Knowing what we don't know is wisdom.»

Network-Discovery

«Knowing stuff is intelligence.
Knowing what we don't know is wisdom.»

399.
«What would your life be like if you only pleased yourself?»

400.
What is the biggest misconception others have about you?

401.
What might contribute to the misconceptions others have about you?

402.
How do the misconceptions others have about you make you feel?

403.
How do others make you feel about yourself?

404.
Where are the kind of people in your life that move you forward?

«Knowing stuff is intelligence.
Knowing what we don't know is wisdom.»

405.
What signals could you have given to others that contributed to your current situation?

406.
If you were to live as someone who takes full responsibility for their actions and feelings without blaming others, what would be different?

407.
If your network was perfect, what's the one thing that would be different?

408.
Has your network worked for you in the past?

409.
Who else is involved in your current situation and how?

410.
Who gave you your beliefs? How do you feel about that person?

411.
What's really important to you in life? Will your network help you achieve more of that?

412.
Who is your audience?

413.
Who are the most critical players in your situation?

«Knowing stuff is intelligence.
Knowing what we don't know is wisdom.»

414.
Write about someone who has helped you become the person you are today.

415.
Who could you ask to support you, and what do you need them to do for you?

416.
Is your network something you genuinely want, or is it something you think you should have?

417.
When you think about your network, what do you feel?

418.
What do you want most in a friend?

«Knowing stuff is intelligence.
Knowing what we don't know is wisdom.»

419.
«When do you give your power away and to whom?»

420.
What does your network allow you to do?

421.
Write down what changing your network will look like in your life.

422.
What would be the most significant impact from changing your network?

423.
Write down how you will handle each day when your network has changed.

424.
How does your network affect other areas of your life?

«Knowing stuff is intelligence.
Knowing what we don't know is wisdom.»

425.
«What would you do if others never changed?»

«Knowing stuff is intelligence.
Knowing what we don't know is wisdom.»

426.
How does what others think affect how you feel about yourself?

427.
Who benefits from you changing your network?

428.
On a scale from one to ten, how important is your network to you personally?

429.
How does your network align with your values?

430.
Does your network align with who you are?

«Knowing stuff is intelligence.
Knowing what we don't know is wisdom.»

431.
What would your best friend advise you to do?

432.
What would you advise your children to do in your situation?

433.
Who drains you?

434.
Imagine you're fully confident that others will support you.
Now, what could you do?

435.
Imagine having a chat with the wisest person you can think of. What would they tell you to do?

436.
If you were an expert in the area of your network, what would you advise yourself to do?

437.
Who could you talk to who would illuminate your issue?

438.
How could you bring more creativity, fun, and joy to your network?

439.
For your network to be perfect, what would have to change?

440.
Who has influenced your life, and how?

«Knowing stuff is intelligence.
Knowing what we don't know is wisdom.»

441.
«How do you teach people, to treat you?»

442.
Think about someone who inspires you. What about them is inspiring?

443.
Where could you be more forgiving and understanding of others?

444.
What would you advise your best friend to do if they were in your situation?

«Knowing stuff is intelligence.
Knowing what we don't know is wisdom.»

Thirty years ago, I switched from the chanting sounds of a catholic convent college to the Ozzy Ozbourne tunes of busy fine-dining kitchens. This sharp turn set the tone for the career that followed. I took a chef's knife, a Swiss accent, and a pair of Denim on a binge through six careers in culinary art, publishing, entertainment, tech & human sciences.

My journey may read a bit like an early draft of a failed Quentin Tarantino script. But for me, my career wasn't so much about the roles I filled than it was about being on a quest for innovation. I admit that I would make for a horrible guidance counselor. But I can assure you that I learned a thing or two about the imaginative potential of ambiguity, the abundant possibility of uncertainty, and some (ugly) truths of creative transformation along my way.

Asking myself the very same question I asked myself 30 years ago when I studied at a convent college: «Where's the fun in this?» And while I may not have all the answers, I have an idea or two about where to start the quest.

J «Fed» Federer

info@jfederer.com

«Knowing stuff is intelligence.
Knowing what we don't know is wisdom.»

www.ingramcontent.com/pod-product-compliance
Lightning Source LLC
Chambersburg PA
CBHW020431220526
45464CB00002B/661